Teacher in Space

CHRISTA MCAULIFFE

Corinne J. Naden
and Rose Blue

A Gateway Biography
The Millbrook Press
Brookfield, Connecticut

From Corinne:
For my very special young cousins,
Christie, Lauren, and Theresa Coquel
and Ricky, Heather, and Justin Coquel

From Rose:
To Rachel with love

Cover photograph courtesy of NASA

Photographs courtesy of NASA: pp. 4, 8, 14, 18,
23, 25, 29, 32, 35, 40, 43; Grace Corrigan:
pp. 11, 16, 21; UPI/Bettmann Newsphotos: p. 37.

Cataloging-in-Publication Data

Naden, Corinne J.
Christa McAuliffe: teacher in space / by
Corinne J. Naden and Rose Blue.

p.   cm.   (A Gateway Biography)
Bibliography p.
Summary: The first private American citizen chosen
to go on a spaceflight, Christa McAuliffe, lost her
life when the *Challenger* exploded just after liftoff.
Describes her special interest in the space program.
ISBN 1-56294-046-5 (lib. bdg.) ISBN 1-878841-58-0 (pbk.)
1. McAuliffe, Christa, 1948–1988.   2. Challenger
(Space shuttle).   3. Astronauts.   4. Space shuttles.
I. Title.   II. Title: Teacher in space.   III. Blue,
Rose.   IV. Series.
B (92)   1991

On January 28, 1986, the space shuttle
Challenger *exploded just after takeoff from
Cape Canaveral, Florida. It was the worst
disaster in the history of the U.S. space
program. All seven aboard were killed.*

*Among them was Christa McAuliffe. Unlike
the others aboard, she was not a scientist
or a professional astronaut. She was a
schoolteacher. She had grown up during the
time when the United States was sending its
first, exciting missions to space. And she had
been chosen to be the first private American
citizen in space.*

This is Christa McAuliffe's story. The
Challenger *explosion was a tragedy. But
Christa McAuliffe is remembered for her
courage, her energy, and her spirit of hope.*

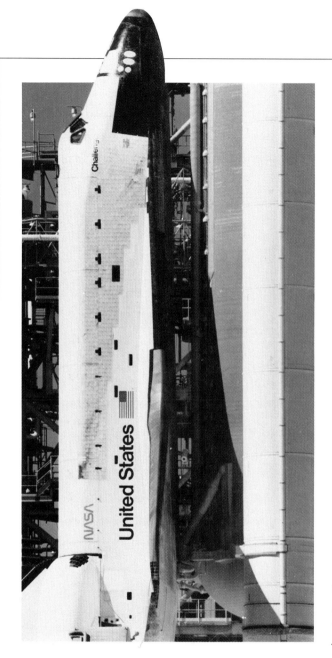

The space shuttle Challenger *on the launch pad at Kennedy Space Center on January 28, 1986.*

Like a giant silver bird, the space shuttle waited on the launch pad. It seemed ready to fly to the heavens. Trails of smoke curled around it in the bright morning sun. The *Challenger* was about to blast off.

At least 3,000 people had gathered for the flight that winter morning. The Kennedy Space Center buzzed with excitement. It was now past 11:00 A.M. The countdown had stopped. Would it begin again? Would there be a launch today?

This space shuttle mission, Flight 51-L, should have taken off on January 23. It didn't. The weather was bad that day and the flight was canceled. Now it was Tuesday morning, January 28, 1986. Still, no one was sure if the shuttle would go.

The problem was weather again. It was clear, but it was *very* cold for Florida. That worried some officials at the Space Center. The shuttle had never been launched in such cold. Icicles were frozen to the outside of the spacecraft. They would break away during lift-off. Could the sharp ice damage the tough but thin skin of the *Challenger*?

Other Space Center people said no. There was

no reason to worry. An ice team would look over the shuttle just before launch. The team would knock all the icicles off. It would be safe.

Some engineers also worried about the cold. The space shuttle has three main parts. The "airplane" part, which carries the astronauts, is called the *orbiter.* It is the part that returns to Earth with the crew. At lift-off, the orbiter rides piggyback on the huge *fuel tank.* Attached to the fuel tank on either side are two *rocket boosters.* They carry millions of gallons of fuel. Each one is fifteen stories tall and is made of steel panels. The panels are held together by rubber seals called O-rings. Some engineers were afraid that the very cold weather might break the tight seals of the O-rings. But others did not agree.

Would there be a launch? Family and friends who were gathered at the Space Center stared at the space shuttle and waited. Inside the *Challenger,* the crew members waited. They had been strapped into their seats since 8:36 A.M.

The United States had already launched 24 space shuttle missions. They all returned safely. This one, number 25, was special. Its crew was special. That's why there was so much excitement that January morning.

Flight 51-L carried a crew of seven. There were five men and two women. Five of them were professional astronauts. Francis R. (Dick) Scobee, 46, of Washington, was the commander. This was his second spaceflight. The pilot, Michael J. Smith, 40, of North Carolina, was on his first flight. Judith A. Resnik, 36, of Ohio, was a mission specialist on her second spaceflight. She had been the second American woman in space. Hawaiian-born Ellison S. Onizuka, 39, was also a mission specialist on his second flight. So was Ronald E. McNair, 35, of South Carolina. He had been America's second black astronaut in space.

The two civilians had never been in space before. One was Gregory B. Jarvis, 41, an electrical engineer from Michigan. The other was a schoolteacher from New Hampshire. Her name was Sharon Christa McAuliffe. She was 37 years old. And she was the main reason that there was so much excitement about this shuttle flight.

Christa McAuliffe was not an astronaut, as Judy Resnik was. She was not an engineer, as Greg Jarvis

The Challenger *crew. Front row (from left):*
Michael J. Smith, Francis R. Scobee, and
Ronald E. McNair. Back row: Ellison S. Onizuka,
Sharon Christa McAuliffe, Gregory B. Jarvis,
and Judith A. Resnik.

was. Except for this flight, she was not part of America's space program at all.

Christa McAuliffe was a schoolteacher, a wife, a mother—the girl next door. She had been chosen from 11,000 other teachers. She was to be the first private American citizen in space.

Now, Christa and the rest of the *Challenger* crew waited on this chilly winter morning. Their families and friends waited. Millions of Americans watched their television screens and held their breath. So did Christa McAuliffe's students back in Concord, New Hampshire.

Finally, the word came. The decision was made. The flight would go!

The countdown continued . . . ten . . . nine . . . eight . . .

This was a countdown to Christa McAuliffe's dream. Christa had thought about space travel since she was a young girl. She had grown up with America's space program.

When *Christa was born* on September 2, 1948, there wasn't any space program. The first artificial satellite in space, *Sputnik I*, was launched by the Soviet Union in 1957.

Sharon Christa was born in Boston, Massachusetts, to Edward and Grace Corrigan. She became known as Christa. The family later moved to Framingham, about 20 miles from Boston. Christa helped raise her four younger brothers and sisters. She grew into a pretty girl with a sunny, friendly personality.

Christa's young years were ordinary. She grew up much like other children in the 1950s. She went to Brookwater Elementary School. She was a good student who worked at her studies. Her second-grade teacher once told Christa's parents that she tried too hard to be perfect. She took piano and dance lessons and she was a Girl Scout.

Christa's sister Betsy remembered: "There was nothing unusual [about the Corrigan family]. We were just a big family—an average family."

Christa's mother was a fashion model, and Christa went to modeling school for a while. She appeared on television in a fashion show. She even won a title: She was named Queen of Saxonville Playground in Framingham.

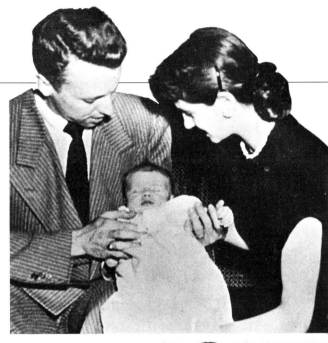

Christa with her parents, Edward and Grace Corrigan, in 1948.

Christa (left) with brothers Christopher (Kit) and Steven and sisters Betsy and Lisa.

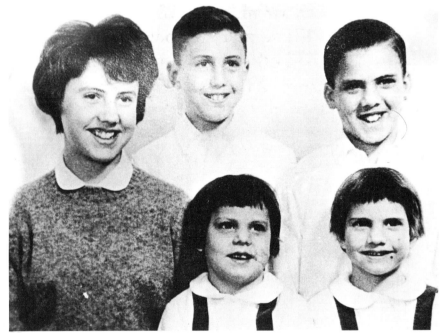

When she grew up, Christa McAuliffe would be chosen to ride the shuttle into space. But when she was a child, she had motion sickness. She could not go on amusement park rides because she threw up!

On October 4, 1957, the Russians shocked the world when they launched *Sputnik I*. They especially shocked people in the United States, who thought the United States would be the first country in space.

Christa was nine years old at the time. She didn't pay much attention to all the fuss. But the U.S. government began to speed up its space program, competing with the Soviets.

In July 1958, NASA—the National Aeronautics and Space Administration—was formed. Today NASA operates all of America's space programs. It has three main locations. Most space missions are launched from the Kennedy Space Center, north of Cape Canaveral, Florida. The Johnson Space Center in Houston, Texas, takes charge of manned spaceflights after lift-off. The Jet Propulsion Laboratory in Pasadena, California, is in charge of unmanned probes into deep space, like a mission to Jupiter.

May 5, 1961, was a big day for NASA. The first U.S. astronaut went into space. His name was Alan Shepard. His flight in *Freedom 7* lasted only 15 minutes and 22 seconds. It did not go into orbit.

Christa Corrigan was excited about Shepard's flight. She was now in junior high school in Framingham. Christa watched the lift-off with her classmates on a black-and-white television set. She never forgot it. She told a classmate that one day she wanted to ride in space.

Space had become an important part of Christa's life. But nearly a year passed before she saw another space shot. Then, on February 20, 1962, John Glenn, later a U.S. senator, became the first American in orbit. He circled Earth three times in the spacecraft *Friendship 7*.

While Americans were still talking about John Glenn's flight, Christa was getting ready for high school. She entered Marian High School in the fall of 1962.

Marian High in Framingham was a small Catholic school for girls and boys. It had high standards and strict rules. Classes were taught by nuns who wore long black dresses with starched white bibs.

Above: Alan Shepard, first astronaut in space. Above right: The rocket that carried John Glenn aloft. Bottom: Ed White floats in space on his famous "spacewalk."

14

The girls wore gray blazers and plaid skirts. The boys wore jackets and ties.

Christa studied hard. She was a happy, friendly, pretty girl with a bubbly sense of humor. She joined many school activities—the glee club and the orchestra, the student council, the ceramics and German clubs. Active in sports, she was on the girls' basketball and volleyball teams. She was an all-star player on the girls' softball team. Christa Corrigan was a busy, popular teenager.

In 1963, during Christa's second year at Marian High School, she met a handsome, dark-haired classmate. His name was Steve McAuliffe. They were both sixteen when Steve asked Christa to marry him. She said yes. Marriage, however, would wait until they both finished college.

On June 3, 1965, the first American walked in space, leaving his spacecraft in a special protective suit. He was astronaut Ed White, pilot of *Gemini 4*. Christa was a high school junior. At the end of her senior year, on May 30, 1966, the United States landed an unmanned satellite, *Surveyor 1*, on the moon. Christa and her friends talked about it. Would someone, someday, walk on the moon?

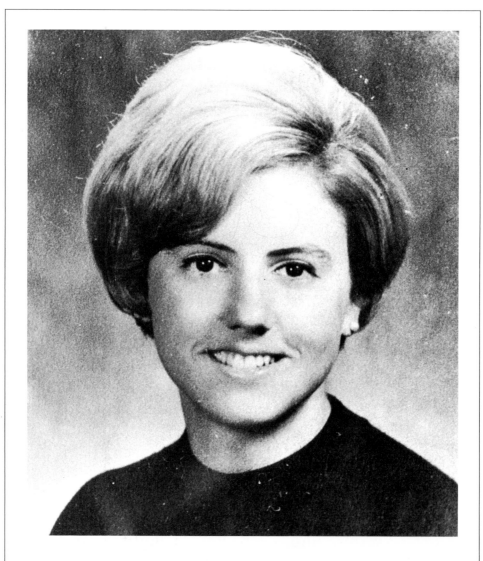

Christa's high-school yearbook picture. She graduated from Marian High School in 1966.

On Earth it was time for graduation. And soon it was time for Christa and Steve to part. Steve went south to Virginia Military Institute. Christa went to Framingham State College. She was a history major and decided that she would be a teacher. In one of her classes, a teacher asked who would like to go to the moon. Christa quickly raised her hand.

In fact, the United States was moving quickly toward the first manned mission to the moon. On December 21, 1968, three American astronauts—Frank Borman, James Lovell, and William Anders—circled the moon in *Apollo 8.* They were the first to see the moon's "other side," the side that faces away from Earth.

Then, on July 20, 1969, Neil Armstrong, on the *Apollo 11* mission, stepped onto the moon's surface. He was the first person to do so. It was a proud day for NASA and the United States.

Christa was still a college student. She was thrilled with the moon landing. She collected magazine articles about Armstrong's flight, and she dreamed. But she also had other things to think about.

Apollo 11 *reached the moon in July 1969.*
Here, astronaut Edwin Aldrin poses on the
moon's surface next to the U.S. flag.

In the late 1960s, the nation was in turmoil. Martin Luther King, Jr., the leader of the civil rights movement, was shot and killed in 1968. So was Robert Kennedy, brother of the late President John F. Kennedy. And many Americans were angry because the United States was fighting a war in Vietnam, in far-off Asia. They said the war was wrong. They wanted American troops to come home. People marched in the streets to protest the war. College students protested on campuses. Some students at Kent State University in Ohio were killed when soldiers fired on them.

Christa did not riot, carry banners, or make speeches. Still, she began to notice what was happening in the world. She and her classmates wore black armbands to their graduation in 1970. It was a quiet protest against the war in Vietnam.

Soon *after graduation,* on August 23, 1970, Christa and Steve were married in Framingham. They moved to Washington, D.C., where Steve went to law school. Christa taught junior high school students in nearby Maryland.

Christa loved to teach. Her enthusiasm and her love of living shone in the classroom. She believed that children's dreams really could come true. She dared her kids to "reach for the stars."

"Whatever it is, try it," she told them. "If you don't like it, don't do it again. But you might find out it's something you love." It was not hard to catch Christa's spirit.

Christa was both teacher and student during those years. She earned a master's degree in school administration from Bowie State College in Maryland. Steve finished law school. Their first child, Scott Corrigan, was born in 1976.

A second child—daughter Caroline—was born to Christa and Steve in 1979. By that time they were back in New England, in Concord, the capital of New Hampshire.

Concord had about 32,000 people and a small-town atmosphere. Christa liked that. The McAuliffes settled into an old three-story house. Steve began his law work. Christa said that she would be happy just staying home with the children.

That did not last long. Christa had too much energy for one job. Soon she was back to teaching.

Right: Christa married Steve McAuliffe in 1970. Below: Four generations of Christa's family. Mrs. James Corrigan, her grandmother, is at left; Mrs. Edward Corrigan, her mother, is at right. Christa is holding baby Caroline.

On April 12, 1981, the United States launched its first space shuttle flight. The *Columbia* returned safely. Christa did not know then how important the space shuttle would be to her.

Just two blocks from the McAuliffe home was Concord High School. Christa began to teach social studies there in 1982. The principal, Charles Foley, later recalled: "Christa McAuliffe was one very good teacher. She was a high energy person. A popular teacher, she was always in control by her very personality. We tell young teachers, 'Get half-way as good as she was and you'll be doing really well.'"

Christa got her students involved. Learning was a real-life experience to her. She made her students feel that way too. She asked state government officials and judges to speak to her classes. She led the students on field trips. They dressed up in period costumes for a history lesson. She staged mock trials to teach law. They studied the ups and downs of the stock market. Christa's kids learned by doing; that was her way.

Christa was busy with teaching and family life, which now included pet cats. Even that was not

The space shuttle Columbia *lifts off on its maiden flight in 1981. The shuttle was the first spacecraft that could return to Earth, land like an airplane, and be used again.*

enough. She joined other activities, as she had during her own school days—the church, the tennis club, the local playhouse. She raised money for the YMCA and Concord Hospital. She was a Girl Scout leader. She jogged. She swam at the country club with Scott and Caroline. She was always busy. That, too, was Christa's way.

In June 1983, astronaut Sally Ride became the first American woman in orbit. Christa McAuliffe, wife, mother, and teacher, was then in her mid-thirties. In most ways she was an ordinary American living an ordinary life. Yet in one way Christa was not ordinary at all. Tucked into the back of her mind was a dream of adventure and an "I-can-do-it, let's-go-for-it" spirit.

Then the chance came to make that dream come true. This is how that one-in-a-million chance happened.

By 1984, NASA had launched several shuttle missions. Now more money was needed for space projects. The government wanted the public to get more involved. Why not send an ordinary citizen into space? In August 1984, President Ronald Reagan announced: "I am directing NASA to begin a

Ch

In 1983 Sally Ride became the first American woman in space. This picture shows her on the flight deck of the shuttle Challenger *during her history-making flight.*

search in all of our elementary and secondary schools, and to choose as the first citizen passenger in the history of our space program one of America's finest, a teacher."

Christa heard the president's message and smiled. So did her husband Steve. "Go for it," he said. They both knew that Christa would apply.

She filled out the eleven-page application. More than 11,000 other American teachers did the same, 79 of them just from New Hampshire!

Ann Tousignant, a graduate of Concord High School, was a student in Christa's last social studies classes. Ann remembered Christa as a good teacher, "caring and friendly." And she remembered when Christa applied for the teacher-in-space mission.

"She was trying for the NASA program that school year," Ann said. "She told her students about it, but she didn't think she'd be picked. She did it as kind of a lark. She told the class, 'I'll try. Why not?' But we were all pulling for her."

NASA asked why Christa wanted to be the first private American citizen in space. In her answer, she recalled watching the early space shots back in junior high school. "I remember when Alan Shepard made his historic flight—not even in orbit—and I was thrilled," she wrote. "I cannot join the space program and restart my life as an astronaut, but this . . . is a unique opportunity to fulfill my early fantasies. I watched the Space Age being born, and I would like to participate."

Privately, Christa felt that as a teacher she could talk to Americans, especially children, about being in space. She would be a pioneer. She admired those pioneers who long ago opened the American West. They were just ordinary people with a dream. Going into space was a little like going into that unknown territory.

Months went by. Nothing came from NASA. Finally, news came in April 1985. Christa was one of the finalists!

Well, that's something, she thought. Maybe I can make it to Houston for the last competition.

In June she was in Washington, D.C.—along with 113 other finalists. "I'll never make it," she told Steve. "These people are doctors and authors and scholars . . ." She said that she felt like one of her students, about to take a final exam.

Christa was asked what special project she would suggest if she were chosen. She replied, "To keep a space journal, an ordinary person's diary just as the earlier American pioneers did when they traveled West."

Ten finalists were picked to go to Houston, Texas. Christa was one of them. She was thrilled, but she still did not think she had a chance.

Christa took lots of tests at the Johnson Space Center in Houston. She rode in a KC-135. This machine is known as the "vomit comet" because riding in it feels like riding on a spaceflight. Christa's hair stood on end as she bounced from wall to wall. But she made it. Not bad for a girl who used to throw up on amusement park rides!

Christa did not think she was the best teacher of the ten in Houston. She did not think she was the smartest. She did know that no one wanted to be chosen more than she did, so she kept the dream alive. "Wouldn't it be wonderful for a history teacher to make history?" she said.

After all the tests and all the interviews, the judges took only a few minutes for the final choice. On July 19, 1985, NASA made this announcement:

Christa (sixth from left) with the other teacher-in-space finalists at Houston. They are standing next to a KC-135, an airplane that can mimic the effects of spaceflight.

"Vice President George Bush today named Sharon Christa McAuliffe, a teacher at Concord High School in Concord, New Hampshire . . ."

"Unbelievable!" said husband Steve. "She did it!" shouted her high school students.

This ordinary American schoolteacher was now a celebrity. Concord named August 6 as Christa McAuliffe Day. She was a guest on television shows. Magazines and newspapers printed articles about her. Yet former student Ann Tousignant later recalled that Christa did not change at all.

"I met her in the supermarket that summer, right after she had been chosen," Ann said. "She seemed as she always did. Just a teacher meeting a student she hadn't seen in a while. You'd never know she was famous."

Christa didn't think she was special. Before the *Challenger* mission, she said, "People come up to me and say, 'I really admire you, but I wouldn't want to do it.' I can't understand that. If you had a chance, wouldn't *you* want to do it?"

NASA chose Christa McAuliffe to show that *anyone* could go into space. A schoolteacher or the girl next door could fly on the shuttle. It chose her for another reason too. Christa was a modern hero. She was a person willing to try the unknown. She had a dream, but she was realistic. She knew that dream could be dangerous. Christa knew what NASA knew: Even with all those successful shuttle missions, spaceflight was a very risky business.

It was time now for serious space training in Houston. That meant leaving family, home, and work. The separation was especially hard for young Scott and Caroline. Christa was often very homesick, but she felt that she was doing the right thing. This was her chance of a lifetime.

Christa did not worry about the hard training. She was, however, nervous about meeting the *Challenger* astronauts. They were professional space scientists. Would they think she was just "going along for the ride"? She wanted to prove that she could work just as hard as they. When the time came, she would be ready.

She did, and she was.

Christa first met the *Challenger* astronauts on September 11, 1985, in Houston. Soon she relaxed. They liked her and treated her as part of the team. She was especially pleased about her friendship

Above: Challenger crew members train in a model of the shuttle. From left are Barbara Morgan (Christa's backup as teacher in space), Christa, Greg Jarvis, and Ronald McNair. *Left:* During training, Barbara and Christa had to get used to the feeling of weightlessness. Here, they practice an experiment planned for the mission.

with Judy Resnik. Resnik was perhaps the most serious of all the astronauts. She was a no-nonsense scientist who did not joke much with the others. But she and Christa formed a warm bond.

Christa also became friends with the runner-up teacher in space. She was Barbara Morgan, a 34-year-old second-grade teacher from McCall, Idaho. She went through training along with Christa. If Christa could not take the flight, Barbara Morgan would go.

There was much to learn. Christa spent hours in a training jet to get used to the feeling of weightlessness. The astronauts practiced moving around in the crowded cabin of the shuttle orbiter. Christa had to learn to eat, to sleep, even to use the bathroom in space.

After long hours during the day, there were training manuals to study. NASA made up problems to see what the crew would do in an emergency. Christa said that did not frighten her. She believed that the shuttle was safe.

The part of training that Christa most enjoyed was planning her space lessons. The first schoolteacher in space planned to do what she did best—

teach. Students all over the country would watch her on closed-circuit TV. This was Christa's reason for being on the *Challenger.* She was a social studies teacher. Better than any scientist, she thought, she could explain what spaceflight was like to young people.

Christa planned two fifteen-minute lessons from space. The first was called "The Ultimate Field Trip." She would give students a tour of the space shuttle. The second lesson was called "Where We've Been, Where We're Going, Why." She would talk about present and future uses for the space shuttle.

Christa was busier than she had ever been during those months of training. She missed her family and went home whenever she could. Her last trip home was for the Christmas holidays.

Finally, *all the training* was over. Now it was January 28, 1986, Tuesday morning at Cape Canaveral. Steve and the kids and Christa's parents were there. Scott was pleased that his mother would be carrying his stuffed toy frog into space.

*A NASA expert helps Christa try on
a helmet for her upcoming flight.*

At 7:20 that morning, the crew heard about the weather and the windchill and the icicles. They worried that the flight might be canceled again. However, the temperature was rising. Maybe they would go. Commander Scobee led them past the crowd of photographers. The astronauts were dressed in sky-blue spacesuits and black boots. Christa was smiling and excited.

Scobee put on his helmet and safety harness. He was the first to crawl into the shuttle. Just before Christa's turn, one of the NASA inspectors gave her a red "apple for the teacher." She laughed and said she'd eat it when she got back.

The hatch was closed. Launch control tested the headsets. When the controller got to Christa, he said, "Hope we go today." She replied, "Hope so too." Those were her last recorded words.

The *Challenger* seven were strapped into their reclining seats. There are two decks in the orbiter. Four astronauts were on the flight deck and three were below them on the middeck. Christa was in the center middeck seat.

The wait seemed endless. Would they go? Would they cancel? At last, the go-ahead signal.

Christa smiles as she leaves crew headquarters and heads for the launching pad on the morning of January 28, 1986. Ellison Onizuka and Greg Jarvis walk behind her.

37

The countdown clicked on. Coming up on 11:38 A.M.; three . . . two . . . one. . . .

A great roar shook the Space Center. The ground trembled. Huge billows of smoke buried the *Challenger.* Then, out of the smoke blasted the silver bird, screaming to the heavens. What unbelievable noise! People covered their ears. They squinted into the morning sun. They gazed open-mouthed at this wonder of modern science. Flight 51-L was on its way!

"Lift-off! Lift-off!" It was hard to hear the voice of launch control above the ear-splitting noise. "The shuttle has cleared the tower!"

Family and friends cheered and hugged each other. Television viewers could not take their eyes from their screens. Higher and higher and faster and faster, the *Challenger* streaked into the morning sky. Christa's students clapped. They were watching their teacher in a scientific miracle of the twentieth century!

Seven seconds into the flight, all engines were normal. The *Challenger* was traveling more than 1,000 miles an hour.

Three seconds later strong winds smashed

against the shuttle. These were the hardest winds ever encountered in a shuttle launch. The spacecraft shuddered and groaned and kept climbing. They were some 35,000 feet up. A little more than a minute into the flight, ground control ordered "go at throttle up." This meant to open the engines all the way, to give them full power.

Commander Scobee replied, "Roger, go at throttle up."

The next and last voice from the *Challenger* belonged to pilot Mike Smith. He said, "Uhh . . . oh!"

Smith had probably seen the orange flash. A small flame first appeared on the right-hand solid rocket booster. Those watching the TV monitors just stared in horror. In an instant the flame exploded into an enormous fireball. It swallowed the space shuttle.

The unbelievable, the unthinkable had happened. At 73 seconds into Flight 51-L, the *Challenger* had simply blown up. It had reached an altitude of about 50,000 feet. Then, streaking through the sky, it exploded. With it went all seven of the *Challenger* crew. The space shuttle just fell

Just seconds into the flight, the Challenger *exploded.*

out of the sky. It hit the Atlantic Ocean at a speed of 204 miles an hour.

At first no one could believe what had happened—not launch control, not the television audience, and certainly not the family and friends of the crew. How could this be?

It took four months for investigators to explain the tragedy. The engineers who had worried about the O-rings were right. An O-ring on a solid rocket booster had failed. The cold weather had caused a gap in the seal. The seal opened and flames escaped. The spacecraft should not have been launched on that cold day.

The whole country was shocked by the *Challenger* disaster. President Reagan spoke to all Americans from the White House. He called the astronauts "pioneers" and "heroes." He had a special message for children, who were especially hurt by the tragedy. What happened, said the president, was "part of the process of exploration and discovery." The future, he told them, "belongs to the brave."

There were many other tributes as the entire nation mourned the seven astronauts. It was an especially sad time for their families. Steve McAuliffe, suffering from shock himself, tried to comfort his young children, Scott and Caroline. He wanted to make sure that Christa's dream did not die with her. He asked educators to keep trying to improve the nation's schools. That is what Christa worked for and wanted.

Christa's students at Concord High were hard hit by her death. Three days after the explosion, 1,400 of them, along with teachers and alumni, met in the school gym. They sang songs, read poetry, and talked about her.

There were no shuttle flights for the next two years. NASA redesigned the O-rings and made other changes to the shuttle for safety. Then, on September 29, 1988, the shuttle *Discovery* lifted off with a crew of five. All went well. The U.S. space program was back on track.

The seven who died in the *Challenger* will never be forgotten. The dream of Christa McAuliffe, ordinary American and girl next door, will never be forgotten either. She is remembered in many ways.

Four days after the Challenger *accident, President Ronald Reagan spoke at a memorial service at the Johnson Space Center. The space shuttle's crew, he said, had "slipped the surly bonds of Earth to touch the face of God."*

Christa was buried in Concord, where the family still lives. The city has opened the Christa McAuliffe Center. It holds workshops for teachers and has a planetarium for children.

Framingham, where Christa grew up, remembered her too. A library there has been named for her.

Christa was proud to be a teacher. In her honor, New Hampshire began a program to sponsor teachers who want to study in a field other than the one they trained in. Many states have scholarship funds in Christa's memory for students who wish to make teaching a career. Christa would have liked that.

Christa McAuliffe was a woman with a dream. She knew that dreams don't always work out. But she knew that often they do. "You can't ever make it if you don't try," she said. "Go for it!"

Important Dates

September 2, 1948	Christa is born in Boston, Massachusetts.
October 4, 1957	The Soviet Union launches *Sputnik I*, the first artificial satellite.
May 5, 1961	Alan Shepard becomes the first U.S. astronaut in space.
February 20, 1962	John Glenn is the first American to orbit Earth.
June 1966	Christa graduates from high school.
July 20, 1969	Neil Armstrong is the first person to walk on the moon.
1970	Christa graduates from college. She marries Steve McAuliffe.
April 12, 1981	The United States launches its first space shuttle flight.
July 19, 1985	Christa is chosen to become the first private U.S. citizen in space.
January 28, 1986	The *Challenger* explodes just after lift-off. Christa and the six other astronauts aboard are killed.
September 29, 1988	Space shuttle flights resume.

For Further Reading

If you want to learn more about Christa McAuliffe and the U.S. space program, here are some books you might like to read:

Christa McAuliffe: Space Teacher by Charlene W. Billings (Enslow, 1986)

Flying the Space Shuttle by Don Wiggins (Dodd, Mead, 1985)

From Sputnik to Space Shuttles: Into the New Space Age by Franklyn M. Branley (Crowell, 1986)

Great American Astronauts by Chris Crocker (Watts, 1986)

Heroes of the Challenger by Daniel and Susan Cohen (Archway, 1986)

How Do You Go to the Bathroom in Space?: All the Answers to All the Questions You Have About Living in Space by William R. Pogue (Doherty, 1985)

The Official Young Astronauts Handbook by Kerry Joels (Bantam, 1987)

One Giant Leap for Mankind by Carter Smith (Silver-Burdett, 1986)

Ronald McNair: Astronaut by Corinne J. Naden (Chelsea House, 1990)

Sally Ride and the New Astronauts: Scientists in Space by Karen O'Connor (Watts, 1983)

Space Lore by Necia H. Apsel (Watts, 1987)

Space Shuttle by Wilbur Cross (Childrens Press, 1985)

The Space Shuttle by Gregory Vogt (Millbrook, 1991)

Index

$20.90

DATE			